100+
First Words
On the Go

Illustrated by

Ailie Busby

Miles
Kelly

On the road

mirror

coach

classic car

TAXI

taxi

top deck

ROUTE 3

wheel

limousine

Which vehicle is yellow?

Some **double decker buses** let **passengers** hop on and off so they can see the city sights.

driver

beep beep

jeep

double decker bus

3

To the rescue

steering wheel

police car

Where do you think the ambulance is going?

ladder

nee naw

siren

lifeboat

lifebuoy

ambulance

rotor
blade

air ambulance
helicopter

Firefighters drive
special trucks to the
scene of a fire.

fire
engine

POLICE

police motorbike

Wheelie wonders

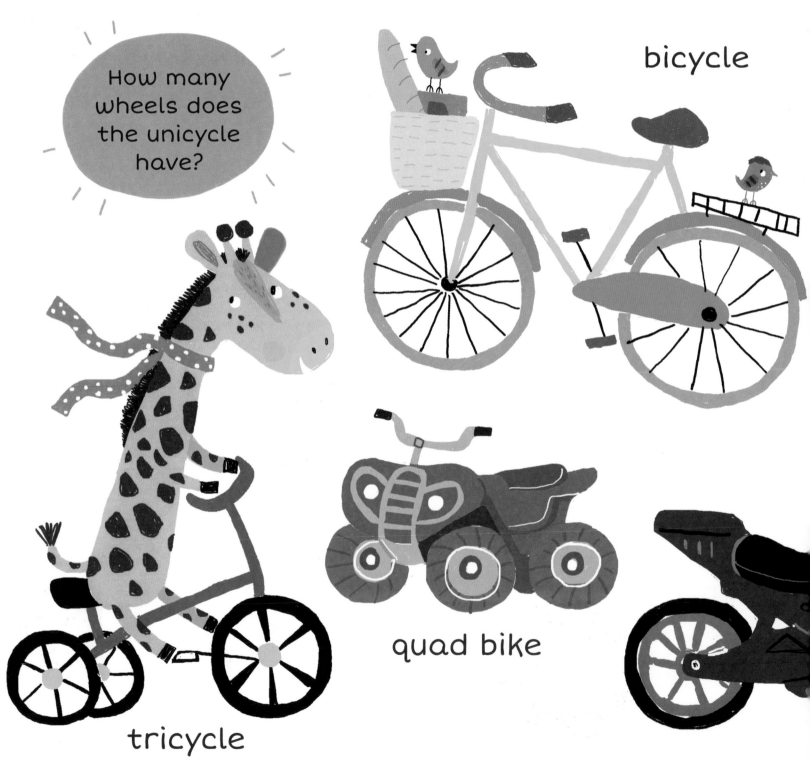

How many wheels does the unicycle have?

bicycle

tricycle

quad bike

handlebars

saddle

mountain
bike

pedals

unicycle

scooter

vroom
vroom

motorbike

A **tandem bike** can
be ridden by more
than one person.

tandem bike

7

In the air

helicopter

parachute

How many aircraft are red?

hot air balloon

jet plane

8

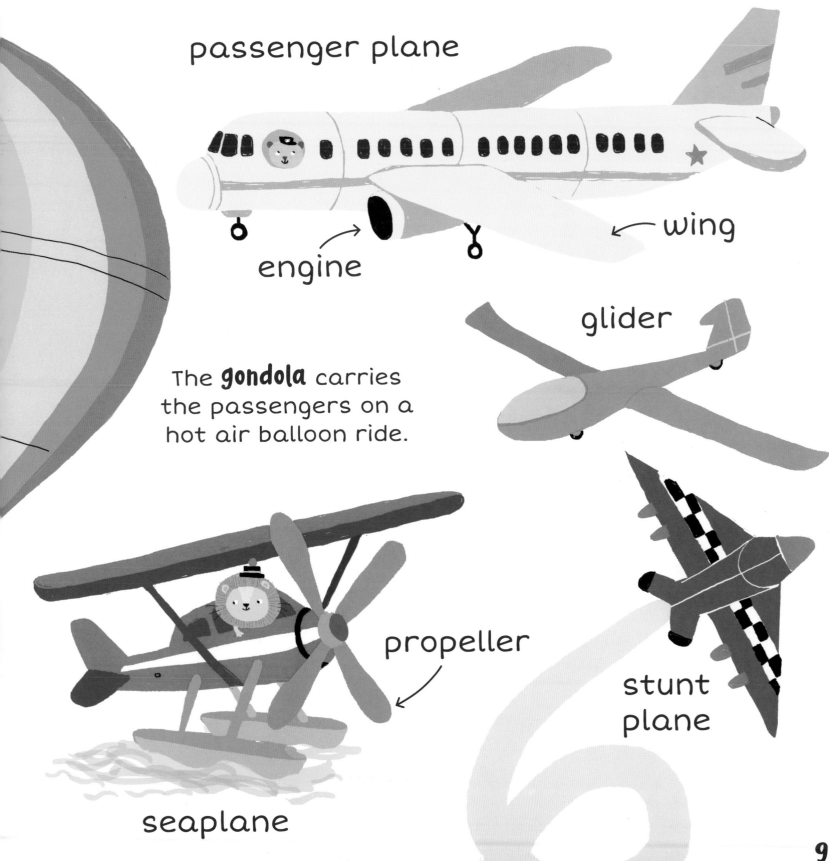

passenger plane

engine

wing

glider

The **gondola** carries the passengers on a hot air balloon ride.

propeller

stunt plane

seaplane

9

Tough trucks

humvee

recycling truck

How many cars can you count?

flatbed truck

car transporter

10

sweeping
brush

road
sweeper

tow
truck

If your car breaks
down, a **tow truck** can
take it to a garage
for repair.

tank truck

Fun time

campervan

recreational
vehicle

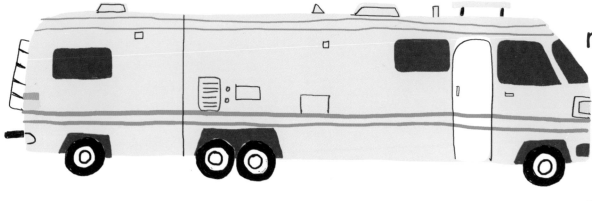

snowmobile

monster
truck

Where would
you go in the
campervan?

cable car

You can stand
on a **Segway** and use
your balance to
travel around.

go-kart

golf cart

Segway

caravan
and car

All aboard

submarine

speedboat

Submarines are able to travel underwater.

fishing boat

jet ski

splash

sail

yacht

What is on the top deck of the cruise ship?

rowing boat

oar

cruise ship

paddle

kayak

houseboat

On tracks

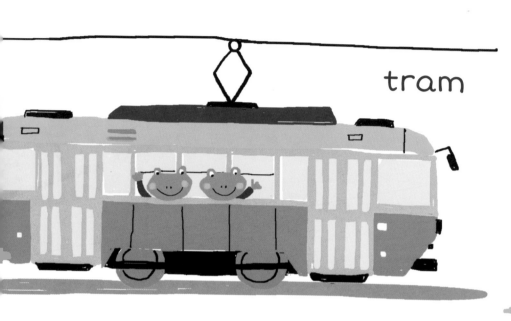
tram

funicular train

Can you find the three crates?

underground train

tunnel

steam train

choo choo

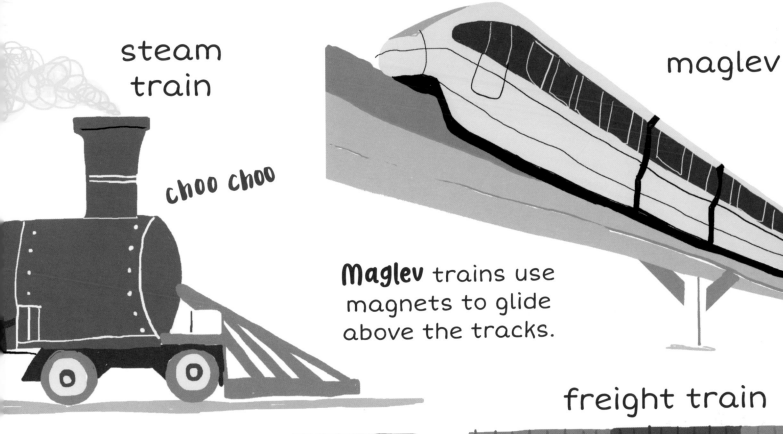

maglev

Maglev trains use magnets to glide above the tracks.

freight train

passenger train

railway track

Working hard

digger

A **digger** is a powerful machine used to dig up and move earth.

caterpillar tracks

forklift truck

dumper truck

Super speedy

superbike

rally car

Which car
do you think is
the fastest?

racing boat

supersonic car

zoom

20

Formula
One car

In a **racing boat** the
coxswain steers the boat
and keeps the crew safe.

paralympic bike

drag car

Farm Fun

baler

bucket

combine harvester

How many sheep are in the trailer?

truck with trailer

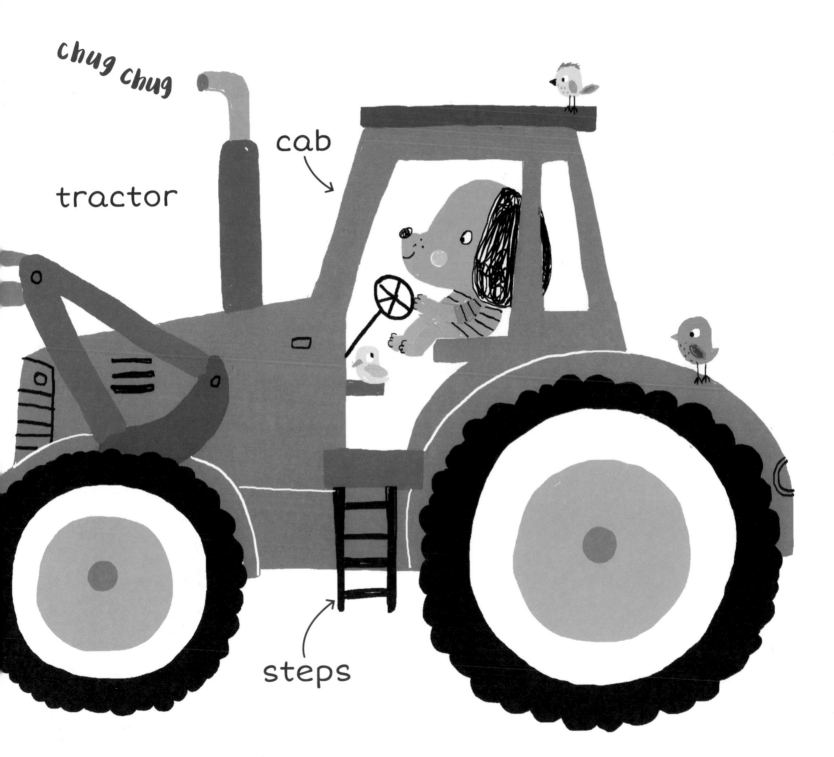

chug chug

tractor

cab

steps

A **tractor** is mainly used to pull other farm machines.

Can you find...

helmet

mudguard

passenger

fishing
net

gondola

funnel

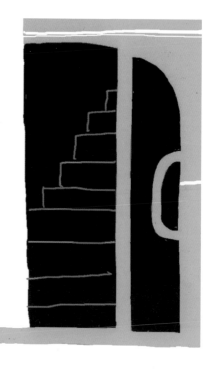

bucket

basket

tyre

rear
platform